Snatched from the Grave

John Ngong Kum Ngong

Langaa Research & Publishing CIG
Mankon, Bamenda

Publisher:
Langaa RPCIG
Langaa Research & Publishing Common Initiative Group
P.O. Box 902 Mankon
Bamenda
North West Region
Cameroon
Langaagrp@gmail.com
www.langaa-rpcig.net

Distributed outside N. America by African Books Collective
orders@africanbookscollective.com
www.africanbookcollective.com

Distributed in N. America by Michigan State University Press
msupress@msu.edu
www.msupress.msu.edu

ISBN: 9956-578-73-8

Table of Content

INTRODUCTION

Snatched from the Grave, the fourth of Ngong Kum Ngong's poetry collections, is an exigent clarion call for a re-examination of self in a society bereft of morals, a society heading for destruction and the grave. It is a skilful rendition in arresting and provocative verse of the redemption story; that Man (Christ) laid down His life for mankind. In *Snatched from the Grave*, like in *Walls of Agony*, *Chants of a Lunatic* and *Strange Passions*, Ngong Kum Ngong writes with an irrefutable, powerful and challenging voice. The poet-persona's experience foregrounds how a lost and sinful humanity can find redemption through faith in the death and resurrection of Jesus Christ. The writer is confident that the transformative, humanistic and revolutionary ends of poetry will rouse some souls to awareness and action by the time they read the last poem in this thought-provoking collection.

Once grave-bound and doomed, the poet-persona after his deliverance, now knows that no act of his or mankind's could have ransomed him except God (Kezeh), his maker's grace and mercy. This is how he puts it in

'You can call me names';
no decree on this earth
no parliament dear folk
can snatch you from the grave.

The poet's sincerity prompts him to confess that his salvation from the doldrums of damnation was an extraordinary expression of love by the 'Immortal Light'. This accounts for the rapturous worship of God whom he sees as a man for all seasons- an unshakeable Rock, 'immutable Godhead', and 'Author of life'. The persona does not care what people may say, his preoccupation is rather with the 'others' who are enjoined to see the 'mess' in their hearts and do something very drastic about it so that they too can enjoy 'life in the fullest free and warm,' whether alive or dead. It is a new life that fears neither the grave nor destruction.

Conscious of the fact that death is the inevitable end of man, the poet's worry is how prepared humanity is for it. Is man created just to live a senseless existence, die, rot and become food for worms? The writer's conviction and belief are that life becomes meaningful only when we take stock of ourselves, recognize our Creator and Saviour and then anchor on His all-embracing generosity. The urgent call in 'Golden Opportunity' for all to 'let not this golden opportunity/ slip through your fingers' is eloquent in this regard. In 'October 16th 1993', the phenomenal day on which he moved from death to life, is vividly recollected. The experience was so memorable that specificities and outcomes become weapons to delineate and celebrate the date. As it were, God used the voices of men to bring transformation in the speaker's life. It was a transformation free of charge, with no strings attached. The collection of poems, serves then, we are told, as a medium to bring people to the saving knowledge of God's grace and repentance. In this wise, personal experience, not theory or academic discourse, becomes the purveyor of vision; a vision geared towards moving others to partake of this blissful ecstasy.

The pathetic appeal, an aesthetic quality of this collection, is a weapon used to cajole others to desist from pursuing vices and vanities or serving the god of ego, the persona too once adored. To live in sin is compared to 'munching dung' and being homeless; homelessness being a metaphor of man's condition without God. In 'Better the Cross', the poet declares that it is better to be crushed on the 'rugged cross' of Christ than accept the 'perishable crowns' of the world which only lead to sure destruction. Knowing that salvation does not end with him, he appeals to all lost souls to avoid the impending crash reserved for adamant souls. From his new pedestal, he adds his voice to his Benefactor's in order to touch the heartstrings of all mankind.

Living in his new status has not been a bed of roses. Opposition has been rife and on the increase. This stiff-necked and obdurate generation has exhausted all avenues to discourage him or destroy his home and family. In spite of the name calling, intimidations, slander, mockery and threats, the poet avers that he can never go back to the dungeon he once belonged to. Many who could have joined him cannot do so because they are people pleasers- wary of the opinion of others, fearful not to destroy the status-quo or are simply being threatened not to defect. The collection is the writer's own way to assure them that he would never stop singing about the advantages of his new found love and the need for others to take that same irrevocable decision to follow Christ. What then would stop him from drumming his experience? Is it trials, temptations, setbacks and disappointments? Since the consoling arms of his Comforter are forever ready to receive all bruised souls, he advocates for steadfastness and stoicism in the face of life's storms. With these virtues, man will not only end at sucking lemons but make lemonade out of them.

The poet-persona might be dressed in his new garb but the fact that he is still human and in the flesh is still problematic. He is often buffeted by sin and even tempted to cast a first stone on infidels. His greatest dilemma lies in his inability to abandon his people or lose his salvation. For this reason, he does not ignore the possibility of another fall if he should succumb to the baits and philosophies of the world. Thankfully, God's grace is sufficient for him. He consequently perceives his cherished transformation as a journey to either enter a boat, a train or just swim to the other side. He is like a river that has meandered through the lanes of vice to a more blissful destination. He invites everyone to undertake that same journey and join him in celebration. No one else but him could have proclaimed with such moving eloquence and infectious enthusiasm those memorable moments of joy he now savours. Anyone hungry for the touch of God will find solace in these poems.

There is a careful juxtaposition of darkness and light, the physical and the spiritual in this work. To live in sin is synonymous with groping in the dark by abandoning the true Light- Jesus Christ. It is prudent for mankind to run to the Light and gain true life and liberty from Death and darkness. Physical man is mortal clay but the soul is imperishable. Gripped by this truth, the poet closes this collection with the confidence that his soul shall live forever. The poet's eloquence is reinforced by captivating images, mind blowing allusions and hilarious descriptions of man's life without Christ. See these: 'condemned goat', 'spineless captive cockroach', 'creaking cricket' and 'rabid rabbit.'

There is no denying that Ngong Kum Ngong has carved a niche for himself in the pantheon of Cameroon writers using English as a medium of communication. As it were, the peculiar and distinctive voice of his poetry, a voice that confronts and moves the reader to action, unmistakably gives him a place of prominence among Cameroon Anglophone poets. In this fourth volume, the poet's wish is for humanity to come to a Father who art in heaven but who is still interested about anyone on earth willing to draw nearer to Him, including even his own 'moribund kinsmen.'

NGASSA LENO KAN
Bamenda, 2010

YOU CAN CALL ME NAMES

You can call me names
if that makes you see
in your reason's eye,
the mess in your heart.
You can even roast me
if that kills the malice
dancing rock in your eyes
but you cannot stop me
from running through my life
to burn the dross in yours.

I have seen strange things
charting my way through
the state nude and rude
knocking my brains out,
straining to figure out
why both freeborn and slave
cannot find rest in life.
I have seen both the rich
and the poor go off course
searching without finding real joy.
I have seen both politician
and the peasant coil before death
seeking without finding a way
to restrain intransigent death
from standing coffins before them.

You can call me names
if that cheers you up.
You can even drink me
if that quenches the thirst
forcing you to disown conscience

for slender slices of stale bread
but you cannot stop me, live corpse
from telling you that what you need
is more than statecraft can purchase,
life in the fullest free and warm.

I have seen silly souls
shy away backward from
the claws of a sick crowd
bending over backwards
hoping to find a way through
this thorny terrain of life.
I have seen both the unfledged
and the grizzled faint depressed,
looking for the foremost pathway
leading away from the graveyard.
I have seen both the decrepit
and the powerful crawl frozen
dodging the jaunty jaws of death,
thinking they can renew their lives
for apartments far from the grave.

You can call me names
if that adds one quill
to the stinking cap
you have worn for years
peddling death in smiles.
You can tear me to bits
to breathe new life into
the contract you bargained
to catch up with power
in keeping with the grave.
You cannot ward off death
with the stroke of a pen.

No decree on this earth,
no parliament dear folk
can snatch you from the grave.

GOLDEN OPPORTUNITY

There comes a time
in life's journey
when one's double
like a dogged deer
pants for a sanctuary
fed up to the back teeth
with the beat of the world.
Such was my landmark experience
when unable to dance Cain's dance
I decided to ditch the world.

In the heat of life
I measured success
with what my eyes drank
and confused survival
with what my tummy tucked in.
I took pleasure in blue jokes
and made lust my bedfellow
yet blue funk always shook me
like a malignant tumour.
I shut the door on hedonism
and struck conceit off my register
to take account of my tomorrow.

Now I see much better
and can fathom the world,
having meandered my way

through lowly lanes of vice
digging hard like a mole
to touch truth with my heart.
I hope to touch your heartstrings
with the eloquence of my drum
and the punch of this unsung song.
I want you whose lives are dustbins
and you eating from golden tables
to drink the waters of salvation.
Let not this golden opportunity
slip through your fingers moribund kinsmen.
Even you famehunting landscape painter
can undoubtedly be snatched from the grave.

DELIVERED

Me
of all the guilty goats
in this valley of death
the blind call nirvana
waiting for the moment,
the time to cross the Styx
lean, toneless and sombre
like a slave starved for seasons.

Me
of all the sentenced goats
tethered in this dungeon
dipsomaniacs call home
waiting for the point of time,
the lightning flash to be gone
young, baited with my boots on.
Me of all the condemned lot

delivered by the Judge himself.

He stopped in my cell
the wrecker of death
smiling, hands wide open
blood dripping from his sides
like rain water from roof tops.
For the first time in my life
I saw the salvaging light
in his gentle divine eyes
twinkle twinkle towards me.
It x-rayed my rotting chest
focused on my throbbing heart
and lifted me from the floor
welcoming and assuring.

Off the world's bait,
I fell on my face
in the hall of life
dullards call prison
waiting for the moment,
the hour to rise to live
like a prince with a scarf
stainless, draped round my neck.
Squeezed out from the jaws of death
I drew a deep breath relieved,
looked around the room joyous
and raised my hands heavensward
delivered from sure destruction.

OCTOBER 16TH 1993

Nineteen ninety three
October sixteenth.
The sun was packing
ready to go to rest
when the birth pains began
in a dim sanctuary.
I was listening to two strange mouths
giving tongue to a salvation song.

I felt a sharp pain
underneath my heart
then an urgent knock
when the song ended.
The pain spread like wildfire
as I eyed the bizarre men
begin another moving song.
They resembled seasoned midwives
giving advice to pregnant women
manifesting signs of delivery.

A force overwhelming,
potent and compelling
grabbed my hand in no time
as soon as the men invited
those who wanted to sing like them
to step forward and be numbered.
I strove without success to balk
wishing I could dissolve like ice
and dribble away unnoticed.
All of a sudden without heed
the force lifted me to my feet,
balanced and shouldered me forward.

I goggled blankly
while the two strange men
struggled hard, sweating
but determined to intercede
to bring forth the babe inside me.
Before I knew what was cooking
the delivery stool turned red,
my heart hurtled over ego,
the lethal scales in my eyes fell
and I could now see beyond doubt,
beyond humanity's frailty
in a world governed by cutthroats.
The two men beamed with merriment
as they embraced me fatherly.
The cords of death around my neck
disentangled and were consumed
as I forsook the road to ruin.

EXTRAORDINARY LOVE

Immortal Light
how deep thy love
that drew a drone like me
from the doldrums of damnation.
I was crippled
but now I walk,
was dumb but now I talk
confounding those who had dumped me.

Your light showed me
the golden gate
through which I had to pass

to savour the dish of mercy.
Fear once shook me
but now it fears,
it howls still but I reign
refuged in the garden of grace.

Wonderful Light
how sharp thy rays
that pierced the beast in me
and scorched its tongue the next moment.
I once wounded
but now I heal,
once tore but now I mend
beckoning on torn hearts to run
and take refuge under your arms
fleeing from the prince of darkness.

Your mercy Lord
pregnant with love
let me off the hook
and offered me genuine life.
Let me dear Lord
follow your steps
reflecting your light
here where every street is dark
and the beast in man dictates
the menu for those in chains.

DESERTION

Finally at sundown
I deserted the gang
like a bruised bull the herd
heading for a place with hay
to lay its head expecting death.
My heart was charged with terror
though the day was unclouded
when I quit to seek refuge
in the refreshing terrain
where I met the stricken Lamb
bleeding but binding the wounds
of those who came wrapped in guilt.
He ushered me in smiling
and bade me take a cushion
very close to His bosom.
Since then I have spurned meanness
and welcomed bigheartedness
for crowns in the palace of life.
I have deserted talebearers,
turned my back on shandy houses
and ceased entertaining Ego
the god I once burnt incense before.

HUNGRY GRAVEYARD

Run this truism
over in your heads,
you who very often
swarm the place like locusts
laying eggs of wreckage.
The wolves you nourish

inside your inside
with the blood of youngsters
and the call girls you kiss
in areas black as night
would someday wolf your guts.
The hungry graveyard will rejoice
feeding fat on rare flesh like yours
save you embrace the Rock of Ages.

Run this fact of life
over in your minds
you who day by day
think nothing but fraud.
The dreams you play host to
in the hotel down town
with the flesh of virgins
and the monsters you hug
in the backyard of night
would without doubt drown you.
The ravenous graveyards will beam
making room for new causalities
save you run back to Elolam
the one who sustains everything.

Weigh your modus operandi
you who breed spiritlessness
like mosquitoes malaria
in stagnant stinking water.
Reconsider all your ways
shifty souls in the dark
for in the distance ahead
I see wobbling mother earth
rising to her feet of lead,
leaping like cracking fire

consuming stubble with relish.
The hungry graveyard will rejoice
eating outstanding meat from earth
but the Light without doubt will lament
the perdition of His handiwork.
Arise and plead for God's mercy
before grace period is over.

THE GRACEFULNESS OF A NEW LIFE

I have tasted the fruit
plucked from the tree of life
and would not mind drowning
in my own blood assured that
my life would not run out here.
I will lie down and rejoice
in the shadow of the hand
that snatched me from the graveyard.

I do not see why
my mouth should not sing
the song that can drain
the bad blood in you
and drown all your woes.
I do not see why
my heart should not flute
under the tree of salvation
piping loud and clear everyday
the gracefulness of a new life.

Better give me vegetables
than mackerel boiled in hemlock.
I am no more master of my life,

no more master of this ugly mass
that would someday rot and be buried,
miserable like a child without roots.
I have tasted the most succulent fruit
harvested from the orchard of Mercy
and would not mind dumping my yesterday
in the yawning pit of hell upon earth.

I have trimmed my fingernails
under the baobab of life
and felt the touch of affection
in the belly of my bosom.
I have accepted my body
be plundered to draw breath again
under the priceless tree of life
where the rainbow of my fate changed.
Now within me glides the light of life
burrowing through my heart, singing loud
the gracefulness of another life,
yes, singing gleeful snatched from the grave.

I WISH YOU COULD UNDERSTAND

Listening to birds sing
skipping from tree to tree
free and gay as the moon
I wonder why I too
more than a match for larks
should not sing my new life.

I wish you could understand
the titbits of my old life.
I am sure someday you too

would sing full throated the song
of the distance you have covered
looking for meaning in living.

The world seductive and sly
would do everything groovy
to prevent you from riding
the horse of your destiny.
I wish you could understand
the eagerness in my voice
so that some beautiful day
you too would sing the story
of the distance you have covered
looking for a swift river
to flush away your dry past.
I wish you could understand
that not even your kindness
dancing in everyone's heart
can save you from destruction.
No person in the whole world
can save you from the Grim Reaper
save the one who overthrew death.

WHY I BEAT THE DRUM

Some bards, believe me
beat the drum loudest
to draw attention
to their ego trip
to cover their spots
and slaughter the swine
that makes them look blue
like barren sweethearts.

Others peal the bells
just to cut a figure.
Still, others beat the drum
for the sheer joy of it
even when the sky is dark.

I beat the drum
to dry my tears.
Yes, I beat the drum
to thank my Maker
and awake from sleep
souls burning to live.
I am not the species
that tastes life-giving sauce
stewed in the pot of truth
but whose tongue darts in and out
like a famished chameleon's
set to snatch some sleepy fly.
I beat the drum for pleasure.

I like to zero in fast
on humanity laid bare
since I have discovered that
death shall never kill my soul.
That is the why and wherefore
this new song invites you all
to turn around just this once
and take a look at yourselves.
Take a look at yourselves countrymen
in the authentic mirror of life,
Christ Jesus, the author of new life.
Take a look around you my kinsmen
and you certainly will discover souls
walking through painted corridors of night

14

bereft of perspicacity and life.
Every now and again I beat the drum
to direct people to the fount of life.

KICK PHILOSOPHY

When I consider how
my youthful years got burnt
running after shadows
before I met the Light
and how darkness strives still
the world to dominate
I urge you to weigh your ways
before the sun goes to bed
lest your spirit be quietened
before the next harvest season
without the real light in your life.

Before I met the Light
foul hands manhandled me
and many dragged to death.
There were times they got mad
and forced thousands to creep
into a store freezing cold
where millions melted like ice
for the upkeep of hell's chief.
I urge you kinsfolk to rise
before the premier cock crows
lest your soul be substituted
before the planting season dies.

Seek the author of life
white wine hid from you

before death beats his drum.
Hide your heart in the light
I pray you knock-kneed souls
to live like true-born princes
sipping the skimmed milk of love.
I survive thanks to it kinsmen
since the Light refined my heart.
Reject the world completely
for the Light to shelter you.
Throw philosophy to the dogs
and spit in the eyes of falsehood
for the Light to light you to life.
Kick philosophy on the arse
for the Light to glitter in you.
Kick philosophy dear men of letters
for the Light to kindle you to candour
and keep you from uncompromising death
hovering hungry around your homestead.

WALK THE PATH TOO.

Beware the bugs out there,
the voluptuous termites
and the fleas in their eyes.
Stiffnecked minds will regret
when the time to live comes
or the fixed day to mount
for room in the kingdom
takes the shape of sunrise.

Scout for the right way through
while the sun in love smiles.
Walk the path traced for you

while you were in the womb
to suck the sweets of life.
I trudge on thanks to them
since the Light lit my heart
and made a man of me.

Beware death in pleasure
plus the lies of the foe
when he grows your greatness
and parades you around
like an unusual species.
The dish he offers you now
and the fame he promises
will in the end impair you,
giving him a free hand to rule
and drown your offspring in faeces.

The ointment on my face,
mixed with perfume from up
plus the light in my eyes
keep bees away from me.
Foul tongues quarter my faith
in the heart of the town
and dogs scramble for my navel
but without notice they grow faint
and worms banquet on their livers
not because I have any powers
but because I now walk the path
retraced for me doubting kinsmen
the day I encountered the Light
and asked Him to be my master.
You too can walk the pretty path
away from the grave to safe hands.

I WILL CONTINUE DRUMMING

You may sniff at me,
unfrock my children
and tear to bits their mum
you who have no faces
when you learn to your chagrin
I am now a new creation.
You may send dogs after me
to bark me back into your world
or tear to pieces my good books
but I will not give up drumming
people to the true source of life.

The morning breath of air
will whistle as usual
and birds will make merry.
Time will drive onward fast
stopping for nobody
and souls without standing
stifled, raped and broken
will continue munching dung
save what has happened to me
takes its course in their lives too.
So I will continue drumming
people to the spring of living waters.

My beholden heart
holds no brief for you
who hold in contempt
those who sharpen the wits.
Sympathy entwines me
like a hungry cobra
each time I think of you

18

locked in your woodenness,
looking for life in the tomb.
Yet you tell me to shut up
though I see you wasting away
with a physician just next door.
You advise me to hold my tongue
though I see maggots in your eyes.
I will continue drumming hard
with the frankness of a cuckoo
till the beats shatter your eardrums
and draw you to the Light of life.
I will continue drumming deep
into the heart of your conscience
till the monster inside you dies.

STICKING ON

I am not unaware
the world will laugh at me
hearing me sing this song
unsung by the redeemed
in the face of persecution.
I know very well that
new fields of fear will sprout
and grow thicker inland
to choke this unsung song
but I will neither tremble
nor pick bones with anyone.

I know for certain that
the pebbles in my shoes
and the bile in your laughter
will make my inside red-hot

19

but I will not shift my ground.
Lightning and thunder threaten
drying up the roots of faith
nurtured robust in the Word
and you, immersed in tradition
have vowed to set my house ablaze
but I will never ever recant.

I am persuaded that
the plot you have tailored
and the venom on the tongues
of those who hate sanctity
coupled with your ignorance
will someday bring tears to your eyes.
Tigers may howl and attack
to satisfy their doomed souls
and assuage their master's thirst.
You may dance your macabre dance
brandishing cutlasses at me
to slash the tongue of honesty
received when I embraced the Light
but I will stick on guaranteed
like a tapeworm in the body.

My foes may soon be here
to choke this unsung song
which often gives them high fever
and causes you lose your temper
but let not your deadly talons
sink into the flesh of the blind.
As for me, I will stick on sure
like a hookworm in intestines.
I will wait till my potter calls.
in the same gentle velvet voice

that pulled me out from pitch darkness
and put this song of life in my mouth.
I will wait in song and celebration
till my Refuge and Salvation beckons.
I will stick on rehearsing my new song.

WE ALL DAYDREAM

We all crave to cross the line
blockading us from mammon
for tongues to pipe our praises.
Oiled zombies pray throughout the night
that their shame may not be uncloaked.

But desire and daydream
have colossal appetites
so do not bare them your heart,
do not play in their backyard
where murkiness meditates
and the master of darkness reigns.

Church and chess I flirted with
in the school of seasoning
to activate my muscles
and sharpen the knife in my voice
in the yawning yard of vision
so that out of aspiration
I could attract your sympathy.

We all crave to be titled men
bestriding our subordinates
but not Him the Light of the world
whose mantle blankets the chilly.

I threw His affection aside
and spat in His sacrosanct eyes
hoping to rise and shine someday
like the sun pregnant with power.
He never ever hated me
even as I strove like an ant
in my dreams to drive into gold.

We all daydream
groping for wreaths
in a world where
the strong devour the weak
and weeping fills the air.
I still daydream
thinking of you,
hoping that someday
you will understand,
return from the grave
and clasp the knees of Christ Jesus.

YOU TOO CAN LAUGH

I remember so well the world
and the Light calling urgently
crossed in combat across the road
leading to the estate of Ego,
sprawled between two dreadful hills.
Garbed in multicoloured garments
I watched them scuffle, confused
my head pounding violently
like a wounded pugilist
charging towards his opponent.
The battle was fierce and frightful

so I slipped away in suspense
but before long turned and looked back
ready to go for anything,
ready to tear down or be torn
but resolved to shatter the mask
I had carried since infancy.

Today I can laugh
not with my eyeteeth
but with my heart ablaze
putting to flight every foe.
You too can laugh in the Light
till your blunt spear is sharpened
to shoot darkness through the eyes
and maim corruption for life.
You too can laugh without fear
and smash the senseless smoke screen
the world has ensnared you with
since you outgrew your mother's breasts.
You too can laugh my kind of laughter
running through storms and broken bottles.
You too can laugh with your heart ablaze
floating in the clouds like an angel
longing to give life to drowning souls.

CHANGE COURSE

How thrilling it is
writing in the light
with assurance just nearby.
To beat time and then lie down
in the healing knowledge that
death is not the end of life

is a song new to some ears.
To serenade for charcoal hearts
with the cemented belief that
humanity can do nothing
to stop breasts mooning after life
from treading lightly close the one
who bid everything into existence
is something to circulate to the world.

How painful it is
watching earthlings
pine and pass away
like dogs without tails.
You are a bewitched dog
for I see you sinking
sitting on your sepsis
alone like an orphan.
With my heart in my mouth
I stare mouth wide open
as you fondle shadows.
Jesus can set you free,
scintillate your pathway
and give you a new heart.

I see you gulping in air
to reduce the seismic steam
steaming your intestines stiff
alone in your wilderness
and my weak eyes swim in tears.
I feel the metal clutches
yet the keen edge of your tongue
cuts through my breast like a saw.
Only Jesus can make straight
the crooked road to your heart

and cancel your contract with death.
I will stick it out to the end
even if this aberrant world
comes down on me like an old wall
and I sink like a lead balloon
so that you can sing the song
 I now belt out prayerfully
for this absurd world to change course.

THE CHOICE IS YOURS

Stew what you like
offspring of the night
in the heart of dryness
if the desert assents.
The eye of earth will blink
at the sight of carrion
and iguanas will weep
unable to weather the storm
tearing through our forests of vice,
rendering the unsaved homeless.

Grow what you want
son of the scorpion
in the belly of earth
if the forest permits.
The tears of sky will drip
like pus from our ulcers
at the sight of groaning
and little ants will sigh
unable to crawl through the rot
driving thousands to destroy self
for an edifice in darkness.

25

Jesus is my witness
and in truth I rejoice.
Once I waddled with masks
writing wry songs for death.
I cannot clown any more
for chameleons clog the place
with the fart of fraudulence.
I will not quench the fire
burning nearest my bosom
eager to light you to life.
I don't want to disgrace the Light
whispering peace deep inside me.

Do what pleases you
offspring of affliction
in the heart of mourning
if the graveyard consents.
The choice is yours swollen head
running after earthy treats
like a peckish prostitute.
The nose of decency will twitch
stung by the stench from your stomach.
Vainglorious folk like you shall faint
unable to face the truth that
life without Christ is meaningless
and that like grass we shall wither.
The choice is yours to live or die
in high spirit or despondency.

BETTER THE CROSS

Better I be crushed
on the rugged cross
the one the Light bore
than soil my soul with salad
dipped in the basin of baseness.
Those filthy fingers of deceit
caressing the bosom of truth
to crucify it the next day
call to mind the lacerations,
the tattered gray stinking garments
you and Darkness, drunk with wickedness
often decorate your victims with
before consigning them to their graves.

I would rather starve
basking in the Light
the one that saved me
than kill my hunger with bread
baked in the yard of fakeness.
Those sly slogans on your walls
arouse millions from slumber
to kiss the backside of Cain
recall the spine-chilling moments,
the time death lurked in the shadows
cuddling the magenta daggers
you and your band of murderers
invented in the heart of night
to swiftly dispatch to the beyond
those who canvas against imbalance.

Better I be crushed
on a rugged cross

and my name erased
from your book of dreams
with a colourless eraser
than brew wickedness in my yard.
I have tasted the sauce of pain
and the chill of night piercing deep
like a lance lancing through my flesh.
I have looked down a gun barrel
plodding through squalor like a pig,
besmearing slothful souls with slime
oozing from the bowels of doom.
Better turn the cross dear friends
before marauding hordes of locusts
ravage your reason beyond repair.
Better be crushed on the rugged cross
than to accept perishable crowns.

RIPE FOR CIRCUMCISION

How long will you resist
spineless captive cockroach
before you look away
from this field of scandal
some people call the world?
Slashing the tongues of foes
to dine and wine with ghosts
like swine at ease in mud
will never bring you peace.
The talisman on your chest
like a chain round your neck
will never allow you see
the rainbow across the sky.

How long will you gamble
naked like an earthworm
in this arena of blood
the dim-sighted call the world
before the earth swallows you?
Breaking the limbs of rivals
to serve agama lizards
will never bring you laughter.
The amulets round your waist
and the incisions on your face
like manacles around your heart
will never save you, little ant
from the thunderstorm in the distance.

How long will you resist
little creaking cricket
the call to salvation?
How long will you reject
little rabid rabbit
the summons to cloud nine
where there is neither battle
nor the craze for dominion?
Deception encrusted in gold
and foulness seasoned in honey
will carry you downstream instead.
Clipping the wings of opponents
to become bedfellows with chaff
licking the bottoms of strumpets
will never give you satisfaction.
Only circumcision in Christ Jesus
will save you from the incandescent flames
galloping feverishly towards you.

REFUGE IN THE LIGHT

Do not frown fallen star
because tables have turned
nor be incensed with those
who pop you in public
like substandard champagne.
The bats shall all vanish
like dew in the morning
and become food for worms
like every cadaver.

Do not fear fallen star
because the sky is dark
nor pierce the eyes of those
who line your path with spikes
for like elephant grass
they shall all char in the sun.
So do not fear facing death
for the Light I have espoused
will contend with your enemies
if you surrender your life to Him.

Do not frown fallen kingpin
because the weather is rough
nor be annoyed with the knaves
who in secret crush your balls
and feast on your fear of death
like bats in the heart of darkness.
On your feet then senescent soul
for your season's end is next door.
Carrion crows eye your intestines
for your demise is imminent
save you take refuge in the Light.

JUMP IN NOW

I hear your days are dusky
and tepid tea burns your mouth
like concentrated acid.
They say your nights are stormy
and mother owl screams hard by
like a woman in travail.

There is a canoe waiting
filled with my Master's mercy
ready to bear you across
without compensation to
where I now live like a king.

When the rains flood the river
separating our kingdoms
I quake with fear thinking of you.
When multitudes drown in the flood
I triple my prayers for you
and the land eroding so fast.

There is a canoe for you
filled with the candy of life,
ready to steer you away
from obscurity to light
without any strings attached.

Jump into the canoe poor guys
to suck the sweets of salvation.
Jump in before profane prophets
clothed in meekness and righteousness,
waving flags of life confuse you.
Tangible life is in the Light

31

whose affection is pure honey.
Nothing in the world satisfies
more than the milk of salvation
so jump in now bleeding brothers
before the sea of stress drowns you.

THANK YOU

Thank you immutable Godhead
that loves a worm like me.
Thank you invincible Saviour
whose gore gushed like a stream
to cleanse my filthiness
and repurchase depraved mankind.
Thank you Light of my destiny
for the peace I now sip
and the fortitude of my heart
in a land warped by crookedness.

Malicious mouths sharpen their fangs
like brandnew cutlasses
ready to slice open my throat
and twisted tongues like snakes
spit venom in my eyes.
I will neither regard with fright
the poisoned arrows in their look
nor neglect the ploughshares
turning over the grass surface
on the field you have given me.

Thank you for the grains provided,
the seasons and the sap,
the courage and the discernment

to plant life giving seeds
no matter the hazards.
I will plough any piece of land
you assign me to, my Fortress,
my Sanctuary and Joy
even in seasons of distress.
I will adjust to concert pitch
the sublimity of your love
in a world teeming with cruelty.

TRANSFORMED

I lived like a grasshopper
flying without direction.
My tongue was like a razor
in the hands of a bitter barber.
I gloried in my folly
and like a distempered mind
I tore up the road of dearth
distributing grains of death.
I also cried for the moon
uprooting roses and rye
from the garden of wisdom.
Though nature wept like a widower
I bolted the gate of emotion
blew pepper into Sympathy's eyes
and fired from behind barricades.
Tremendously bright was my spirit
watching my enemies die like mice.
I thought I had mastered my destiny
and captained the fate of perversion
beyond the limits of our wasteland.

In the tight clutch of death
in the midst of splendour
I wept like an orphan,
chirruped like a cricket
and stooped to see the next day.
I scintillated with wit
and sang like a canary
but got no red carpet treatment
until that phenomenal day
that extraordinary day
that day beyond my wildest dreams
when the Light set alight my dross
and offered me brand-new garments.
Though you debunk my experience
I feel high in my new outfit
transformed beyond what tongue can tell.

SINCE I CROSSED OVER

Since I changed camp
dogs growl and snarl
assembled in the square
each with a kingsize bone
from their masters' canteens.
They want red meat
not stinking bones.
They want gin and whisky
not ovaltine and chocolate.
Since I crossed over to this mansion
they have given me no breathing space.

Times without number
they return at dusk

and congregate near my new home
blown with the bile of blighted hopes
bent on roasting my new spirit.
They want hegemony
not empty promises.
They want freedom and liberty
not spineless speeches and slogans.
Since I crossed over to this side
they have declared war on my household.

Since I crossed over
to savour new life
vipers in guerrilla gear
each with a deadly weapon
forged in the bowels of wickedness
lie in wait for my converted soul.
My case is in Papa's court
yet I must embrace my foes
and wipe clean their running sores.
Since I crossed to this other side
bats have multiplied their onslaught
determined to eat my entrails
and pour out my blood like palmwine
round their houses for libation.

UNMOVED

Day after day
I light my lamp
when darkness falls
and chew the word
when worried and faint.

Without a shadow of doubt
the enemy never faints
and the talons of the night
deadly as a cobra's venom
sink deep into unpurchased flesh.

Snatched from the jaws of death
I am grateful to God
for the lamp glittering
and my elephant skin
that absorbs all punches.

Bending over backwards
in the firm grip of pain
I have not given up.
Under the harshness of stooges
I have by God's amazing grace
been able to endure their strokes
resisting decay erect, unmoved.

The mirror maintains
my head is bloody
my eyes filled with dust
but they stand erect
lifted towards the light.
It matters not what you think
let alone the sickening words
flowing from your mouth uncontrolled
like water from a broken pipe.
I am the upshot of God's grace,
snatched from the grave to the minute.

KILL THE BEAST

I slew the beast in me
turned round and faced the sky
ready to go the way
my new master has mapped out.
Though the pathway is narrow
and many quench on the way
I will not unlace my shoes.

Beyond this lunar landscape
is a lush metropolis
where the citizens carol
day in day out songs of praise.
Though the hurdles are horrendous
and many their members fracture,
I will from my new fountain drink
and lie down calm when darkness falls
though the enemy never rests.

If I fail to awaken
when the cock crows many times
or sleep the sleep of the just
only those in my boat steadfast
should bury me without trumpets.
If you too want to enter life
kill the parasites in your system,
leap the brick wall of duplicity
and bludgeon the bloody blistering beast
that keeps on deceiving you with whisky.
Kill the monster out in the open
before darkness overruns the world.

I BELIEVE

Eyes sticking out
like a sore thumb
gaze unblinkingly at me
as I amble through the day
dressed in resplendent garments
counting the bones in our streets,
thinking of the death in your eyes
and the fright of killing tradition.
I believe things will change course someday
if fallen mankind runs back to Eden.

Beyond your fear
looms ignorance.
Tradition is very good
but the bad blood in its head
irritates the prime mover
who in His infinite mercy
allows the repentant to live.
I crossed to this side of the stream
when I came face to face with Truth,
when the storms of the underworld
and the teeth of slings and arrows
congregated to rampage the world.
I believe the world will change someday
if mankind has eyes only for God.

The other day at dusk
I caught the moon naked
peeping out from behind a cloud.
I thought about you and all those
who spot no spots on tradition
and burst into tears like a babe.

Tomorrow may crush your spirits
save you turn your backs on babbling
and settle matters with Yahweh.
I believe down to the ground that
like a wellgrounded chameleon
you can your destiny reorder
and plug the holes in your intestines.
I believe deep in my inner man
you can wrestle with iconoclasts
and emerge from beneath born again.

CAST THE FIRST STONE

You may get the feeling
I eat eggs every day
since I became a new creation.
There are moments when
hunger dogs my footsteps
like a hunter tracking a squirrel.

I still tussle with my thoughts
to sit and watch indifferent
the belly of Guile grow fat
in the name of affection
or puncture it with a dagger
for the sake of life hereafter.
There are some dry evenings when
thirst threatens to drink my blood
and offer my bones to cabbalists
pounding belladonna in the night
to undo souls seeking salvation.

You may conclude wrongly

I no longer look back since
since I changed position.
Anger and bitterness
still push me into mud.
I still wrestle with my spirit
whether to thrive like parasites
on the sweat of innocent souls
or open my mouth without limit
and cast the first stone on infidels
to show the world I am converted.

I am persuaded
beyond reserve that
like tongues of wild fire
licking up dry grassland
you and I countrymen
under the same banner
safe in the hands of Christ
will the whips of antichrists withstand.
Cast the first stone on indecision
to swim safely to this side of life
then you will know the truth about me.

MY ACHILLES' HEEL

You quake in your shoes
and sigh like flotsam
afraid to join me.
The sun sobs sick at heart
and the air is unwholesome
infested wih lice and rot.

My senses with sorrow simmer

each time I come across your likes
talking about life without life.
Cramps take me captive whenever
I venture to uncork my mouth
to save our people from drowning
when the boat of vice capsizes
for you still lay siege to coquettes
near oceans of putrefaction.
I am stunned by what you consume
and scandalized by your stiff necks.

My heart in consternation writhes
unable to grasp what you want.
The garland I have been weaving
for your head hoping for the best
and the rapture I promise you
give me sleepless nights, my Achilles' heel.
As a woman expecting a child
and within an inch of giving birth
labours and screeches in labour pangs,
so do I swollen with shooting pain
as I contemplate you dice with death
wondering whether I should lose you
or the fertile life I now enjoy
going to bed and waking in Christ
free with feet not touching the ground,
yes, free and happy as a king.

STORMY WEATHER

It is stormy this morning.
Lions stampede in their dens
confused and shaken by fear.

My body is sick with grief
and nausea settles upon me
each time I visit the palace
dodging storeys of skeletons.

I am worried by the storm
and worked up by the lightning,
the thunder and commotion,
the screams and false confessions
in the backyard of innocence.
Reason falters like a drunkard,
the fangs of perversion scare stiff
but the people I invite to live
prefer to drown in drums of dread.

It is still very stormy.
Beetles gather in their holes
put off by humanity's storms.
The storm outside is merciless
but you can outmanoeuvre it
despite the fiery thunderclaps,
the lies and death in golden plates,
the debunking and decision
to finish the faint with fiction
even when their swansong is just.
The Light whose steps I strive to follow
can clamps put on inclement weather
and like forest fire devastate
the storms that compel you underground.

DYED IN GRAFT

Hearts dyed in graft
dance out of step
pockets bulging with loot.
Any attempt to discard
or cultivate new customs
is like stitching your grave garb.

We have given birth to scamps
whose tables are overlaid
with the vomit of kickbacks
in this land of skin and bones.
Any attempt to express doubts
or lead them through salvation lane
is like inviting swarms of locusts
to invade a flourishing farmland.

The lantern of the graceless
shall someday be extinguished
and worms shall mature on them.
Their lips like those of strumpets
though dripping honey today
to seduce and strangle souls
wrestling with indecision
cannot stop calamity
nor derail disaster from
sweeping over them like a whirlwind.

Hearts dyed in graft
can dance in tune
pockets bulging with fruits
plucked in confession and love
from the tree of life and strength

on which Christ was crucified.
Stop fraternizing with Graft
lest you miss the train to life.
Stop setting snares for others
lest the teeth of affliction
chisel deep into your flesh
and the anguish of the grave
come upon you like a bandit.
Hearts dyed in graft can be ransomed.

STILL HUMAN

Though already inside
on this side of the grave
I still feel the power,
the antennae of sin
and the fingers of deception
caressing the chin of my thoughts.
They grow mushroom toxicity,
their viciousness has no limit
and the winds are blowing too low
whistling refrains bereft of hope.
I still accurse when afflicted
and cry when horror hammers hard.
In the crushing grip of slander
even on this side of rebirth,
rage often tarnishes my breast
but the balmy hands of Jesus
always melt the spleen in my heart.

I am still flesh and blood
on this side of the grave
where you won't believe it

hawks peddle human bones
and men must stoop to breathe.
Backscratching has taken root
in this part of mother earth
where one must embrace the Light
to deaden the pain of scorn.
Monstrosity has grown roots
and mouths with scorpion tails talk big
but wallow in their excrement.
I cannot really understand
why I should not persecute them
when the man in me gets angry.
Without the presence of the Light,
the fear of the author of life
and a humble acceptance of guilt
you should never hope to be happy.
I still cannot really understand
why my transformation frightens you.
I am still human dressed in new garb.

MY ATONEMENT

The lily withers
and worms feast on it.
I too shall fade and fall
like dead leaves from a tree
and worms shall throw a party.
But I shall live forever
though you question my conversion.

The world wheezes in pain
and the earth is thirsty.
I too breathe hard and thirst

like a mountain climber.
The way ahead terrifies
and the people around me
leaning on their wisdom scoff.
I have a valid insurance
though you believe I am an ass
seated on the laps of Jesus.

The air is stuffy
and people are scared.
I too snuffle and choke
like a greedy father.
My tears flow like a stream
and sometimes I am worn out
like an overused garment
but I have an antidote
though you think I am foolish.
I am afraid the snakes next door
would undo your expectation
of winning the battle of life
if you don't purpose in your heart
to come to Christ Jesus, my atonement.

IN THE STORM BUT…

The storm still rages
like and enraged sea.
Trees bow grudgingly
and litter leaps in joy
as the wind like a king
walks through conquered kingdoms
subduing the stubborn
and promising hard times

to those who refuse to bow.

The storm rages on
like a hungry beast.
Animals shiver
and children whimper
dismay on their faces,
all scrambling for safety.
The piercing plaintive cries
of insects struggling to escape
meet but with treacherous thunder.

The storm still rages
like a dethroned chief.
Man in solitude moans
and in silence succumbs
in the heart of darkness
as the wind like a terrorist
terrorises nature and life
in this world of dung and refuse.
Why do you still reject the Light?
I am in the storm not broken,
near the valley of death not lost
for my succour is in the Light,
Christ Jesus, the tangible rock
on which I stand unshakeable.

HANDICAPPED

Oh, that my people,
my gormless kinsmen
were a colony of ants
and my tongue a screwdriver

I would screw them to reason
and drive their spirits to moot.
I would sprint to buttress them
whenever they question why
mankind has become so heartless.
I would rend the air in public
for the fallen and the moribund
without renaissance, without prospect.

Oh, that my children,
my priceless offspring
were a team of eagles
and my abode elevated
above the muddle of this world
I would ginger up their mother
and infuse their hearts with mettle
that they may revive the dying.
The people I pinned my heart on
thinking they would opt for the Light
have become as callous as stone,
my kinsmen obstinate and brutal
burying their bald heads in the sand
like ostriches in a wilderness.
Oh, that my people were born again
we would like an army of locusts
descend and devour the plantations
where multitudes have died without hope
and embark on planting redemption seeds.

SINGING FOR JOY

Daily for joy
I sing serene
even in agony
thinking of my new life
and the sweetness therein.

Mankind wanders through life
garbed in strange reveries
looking for great fortune.
My clansmen have lost out
chasing wealth, building castles
without the one who gave them life.

When I sum up my village
and add other ethnic groups
to find the total of our dreams
I shudder to total the future.
Goose pimples invade my whole body
intent upon arousing conscience
to burst into tears of dejection.

Your dreams countrymen
are empty castles
infested with rats.
They vanish overnight,
flit into nothingness
but give your kin sleepless nights
because you have banished Christ,
wedded the daughter of Sibyl
and twisted the necks of thousands
to shut the door on defection.

Though you have hired
on the ball marksmen
with heads like acorns
from lands of ignoble hearts
to moderate freedom this way
brewing venom for stubborn souls
I still rejoice wrapped in the Light.
I sing for joy despite dead ends
in this world so wild, so wicked.
I sing impregnated with hope
calm and confident in the Light
even when the anger of chiefs
promises one death by drowning.

LEMONS OF BELONGING

You have brought me thus far
through the marshland of life
to contemplate deep the realm
and the beauty of your kingdom.
I do no merit your love
I who once savaged your saints
and dragged your name in mire
like Saul at the peak of madness.
I do not deserve your mercy Lord.

You have given me life
and kept my heart heated
in the coldness of this world
I whose coat of righteousness
like filthy rags makes you sneeze.
I do not deserve your grace
I who mocked you on the cross

your blood dripping gently down
like sweat from a labourer's face
to procure for me eternal life
sucking the lemons of belonging.

You lifted me out Lord
from the trashcan of rot
to the threshold of bloom
to blossom on your Word
and lead lost souls to life.
My days of doubt are over,
no more the charm of champagne
no more the charm of intrigues.
The craving to crush every foe
and the dream of lording are dead,
dead and buried under the cross.

I want to grow tough
and burgeon skyward
rooted like iroko.
I want to mushroom heavensward
and bear fruit like a pawpaw tree
planted by gushes of water.
I want you to cross over too
for my bliss to be bellyful
sucking the lemons of belonging.

ARROW IN MY HEART

Kindness is so rare
and love so thorny
these end times that
I worry when people

carved in the image of God
sponsor others to lash life
out of those who can't compromise.
They huff and puff in casinos
like cocks strutting hindermost hens,
snakes in the grass cooking carnage.

The cutting edge of spleen
and the daggers of wrath
waiting concealed in firmness
for Nemesis to draw daggers
grow impatient with big babies.
Those who endorse bestiality
in the name of philanthropy
giving suck to amoral kith
these end times worry me to death.
Their wickedness wears out the mind,
tightens the condemnation noose
around the necks of my people
and makes my relations hesitant.
That is the arrow in my heart
piercing deeper every moment,
gathering thistles and needles
to spread out on the only way
I have chosen to make you see,
the only dependable way
to snatch you from the hungry grave
eyeing you with so much relish.

MY CHASSIS

Something inside my inside
coupled with ass appetites
rise up crimson and tempestuous,
armed to the teeth for collision
with the vendors of illusions.
I feel like a deflated balloon,
incapacitated but sanguine.
Selfseeking impudent desires
plus benighted resolute passions
mount pressure determined to vanquish.
Like ravenous omnivorous beasts
and insatiable grabbing scorpions
they desire to be fed with lymph,
hoping I will satisfy their greed.

I will lowliness breastfeed
and throw disdain to the dogs
barking in the heart of night.
Though I feel broken glass pains
and have the sick feeling that
the emptiness in my bowels
would stand me before Jezebel,
I know my enemies will fail.
The battle declared against me
and the daggers drawn in their eyes
since the Light took over my soul
though bloodthirsty, will not crush me.
They proclaim I am an orphan
without a fruit tree to lean on.
No wonder they have signed a pact
with jinns to crush my testicles
unaware like every foul foe that

...age of all men is my chassis,
the foundation on which I have built
and the mainstay of my tomorrow.

CRASH ODOUR

The reek of crash
saturates the air
turning and twisting
through festering streets
littered with split lips.
The suffocating stench
tears into my nostrils
and struts through avenues
lined with moribund souls.
From gutters deep and dim
dry bones cry out for help
but not a soul pays attention,
no one wants to be left behind
in the dog eat dog pitched battle
for spineless fame on planet earth.

People top their lungs
in strain and red eyes
farflung from the truth.
A river of drowsiness
surges within captured minds,
courses through virgin bosoms
washing bare their consciences.
The drama drives me up a wall
but my kinsmen do not bother
though I pray for their salvation.
The battle gear in their grey eyes

and the oath taken to strangle me
catch the eye of my passion instead.
But no one seems ready for freedom,
no party wants to wear my lenses
for fear of discovering the flame
they fear would destroy the status quo.

The dung of decay
unhinges reason,
deranges the mind
and cruises down streets
teeming with stiff souls.
The mess punches the heart,
whips tense the emotions
embracing those who fall
but holding up to shame
your sidesplitting attempts
to get the better of Death.
Foetuses groan in pit latrines
but no soul shows any concern.
Nobody wants to kiss goodbye
to the gods of fleeting pleasure.
Life without its giver tastes bitter
and stinks like an incurable sore.
Listen to the voice of life calling
to circumvent an eventual crash.

LEANING FULL WEIGHT

I have at long last
learnt to lean full weight
on Christ my Retaining Wall
and beyond doubt the true Light.

When darkness casts the first stone
I spit scorn deep down it's throat.
Like the sun sailing bright-eyed
across the sky sound as a bell
 comes the assurance comforting
like a millpond so fascinating,
the restorative voice of my Lord.

I have once for all
learnt to bank my all
on Jesus my Redeemer.
When fake prophets lead astray
I dare them to battle hallowed.
When all around me is darkness
I hold tight on Him like Jacob
thinking of His refining blood.
Then comes resplendent victory
sweet like honey from the mountain
the reward of living through faith.

I have at long last
learnt to switch on full
the light from the Light
the Dyke of my salvation.
When storms and demons gang up
I repose composed in the Lord
waiting to wake up fortified.
When the amoral world attacks
I chuckle unshaken in Christ
thinking of everlasting life.
Then comes the victory soft like wool
the denouement of leaning full weight
on Christ my certain Retaining Wall.

MATURITY

A malignant growth
thickens in my throat,
grows into maturity
in the twinkling of an eye
and darkness begins to fall
in this land in labour pangs.
Suddenly the deadly node melts
like wax before a frantic flame.
Sinister terror grips my mind
though I possess a brandnew heart
hatched in the heart of wickedness
where gathered with millions condemned
I waited with patience my turn
to step forward and be numbered.
Feverish feelings flaming redhot
and the feeble face of failure
dripping with high hopes despite pain
parade the streets of my being
as I master my plaintive throat
girding my loins for a harvest.
The wind telecasts uprooting
and heaviness rushes upon me
fiercely like released walled up water
but cannot mildew my desire
to slake my thirst with living water
drawn from the well of eternity.

LOOK BEYOND YOUR NOSE

Do not, heart of stone
misconstrue my stance
on my pedestal
nor undervalue
from the depth of lostness
the velvet coat on me
though you and ignorance
have crushed the balls of Truth
and hold thousands captives.
Do not think you are powerful
having rendered many hopeless
and established your reputation
at the expense of bereaved comrades
for you refuse to look beyond your nose.

Though on my pedestal bright
I still snap out stammering
as I garner fragments of self
from a world worn out by distress
and crowds that evil has blinded.
I will not fold my hands and watch
even from my summit of joy
the destruction of hearts so dear.
I cannot keep my stitched mouth shut
even when the fire of youth
and the tears that often tore me
no longer feed the beast in me
that used to wring the necks of fools
because I can now look beyond my nose.

The light around me now
more than ever before

longs to light your path too.
Why labour in obscurity
and perish embracing darkness?
A mighty destructive torrent
is sweeping away everything
and stormy moments multiply
in the wasteful womb of wishes.
My heart will rest upon the Rock
I have chosen for foundation.
From my pedestal assuring
I will stand staring in sorrow
the irresistible current
stripping bare your stunted wishes,
feasting full on your naivety
just because like a blinded ass
you refuse to look beyond your nose.

SWINGING LOW

When from the podium
I slip and tumble
exhausted and weak,
I sulk in silence
swollen with self-digust.
The vagabond in my blood
leaps like a tadpole for joy
intent upon putting to the sword
the voice clamouring for forgiveness
just when off the podium I swing low.

When Ego capitulates
and the wind lashes my face
I stare in silent sorrow
at sir humbled Psyche and sigh.

Am I saddened and broken
because foemen saw me fall
or saddened and tormented
because I have grieved the one
who ransomed me with His blood
or because off the podium I swing low?

You may giggle
but I mean it.
There is neither name
nor peace in pieces.
I purr with pleasure
looking for a place
like a cat with a rat
to sit alone and sing.
I cannot embrace the rabble
nor kiss the posterior of dogs
to burn and burn without ceasing
in a fiery furnace for fools
faking love time over again.

When the world pursues me
like a serpent a toad
I look for a mattress
and lie down below the cross
for new insight and vigour
to punch and knock to the ground
the high priest of butchery.
Swinging low can extinguish
the lantern to light others to life.
I will not embrace obscurity
nor get sucked into a conspiracy
to groan lame in an abysmal pit
even when I am swinging too low.

LIFELONG SATISFACTION

I have laid down sick Ego
like some sacrificial goat
on the altar stone of Faith
having no doubt that someday
my new life in Christ Jesus
will affect not only poets
but political beasts as well.

I have come to know that
there are hunters in the field
but their mission will not pay.
I have found love without strings,
genuine love with no lipstick.
There is nothing I rate more
than the handshake from my new love.

I have left bizarre longings
sprawling naked in the dust
and washed my hands over pride
my feet not touching the ground.
If anyone lays claim to my love
it can only be my latest love
pregnant with affection that no one
bent double under guilty feelings
would afford to dismiss out of hand.
I have found lifelong satisfaction
and the stillness only water knows.
If you want to enter life alive
and blossom before becoming dust
do so before darkness draws its curtain.
If you desire comrades to be snatched
from the voracious grave behind your yard

set your face against mundane hankerings
to drink from the spring of living waters.